TRIASSIC TERRORS

ISAAC LENKIEWICZ

NICK CRUMPTON

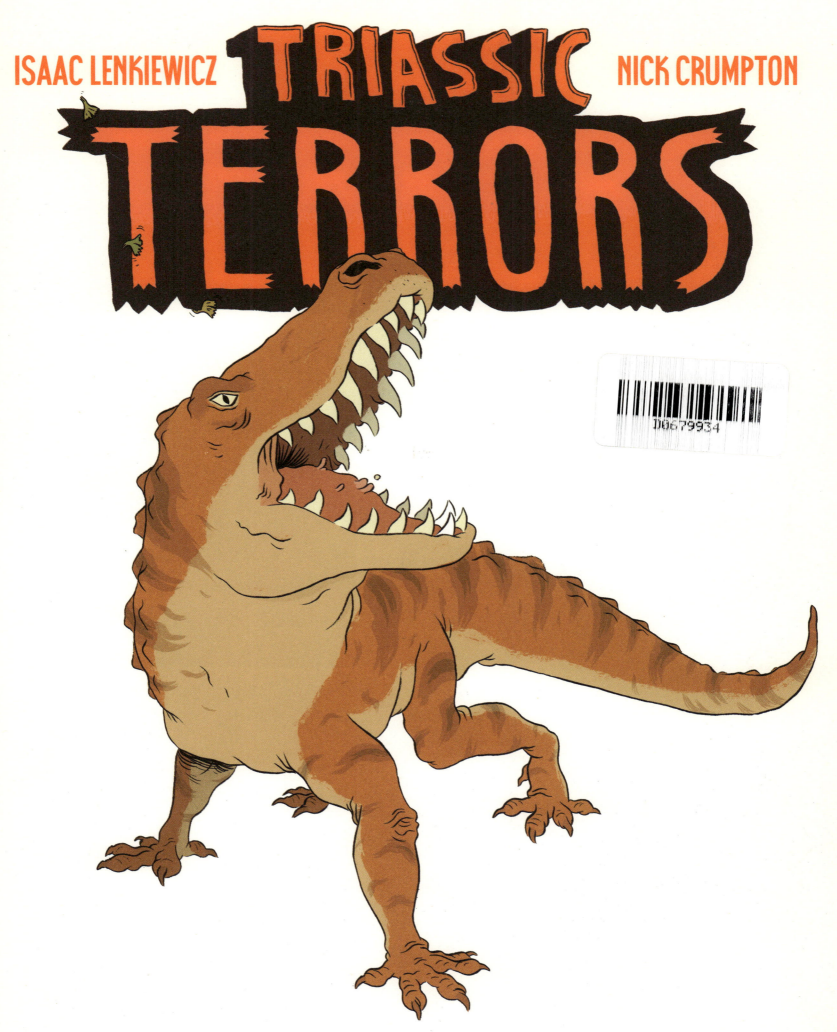

FLYING EYE BOOKS LONDON

WHAT IS THE TRIASSIC?

The **Triassic period** was a time stretching from 250 to 200 million years ago (mya), when the first **dinosaurs** evolved. It was the first period of what we call the **Mesozoic era** (250 mya to 65 mya).

Pangaea

During the Triassic, the world looked very different to the way it looks today. The **seven continents** were all part of one huge **supercontinent** called **Pangaea** which means "all Earth" and there was one huge ocean surrounding it, **Panthalassa**, which means "all sea".

The Triassic landscape was dominated by a group of reptiles called **pseudosuchians**, which looked a lot like crocodiles; the **synapsids**, which were survivors from the **Permian** period and were the ancestors of mammals; and early dinosaurs, like *Eoraptor* and *Nyasasaurus.*

EXTINCTION AND SURVIVAL

The **Triassic period** was one of many **periods** within several **eras** of Earth's history. Some of these time periods ended with events called **mass extinctions**. This means a time when life on Earth was threatened by a **catastrophic event** that caused many species of animals and plants to die. The Triassic followed one of the greatest mass extinctions of all time, when up to nine out of every ten species on Earth became extinct. Scientists call this event "The Great Dying". This could have been caused by many things, a drastic change in **climate**, a **meteor** striking the Earth, or greatly increased volcanic activity.

On this page:
1. Edaphosaurus
2. Gorgonops
3. Diictodon

On the horizon below, draw and colour what you think might have caused the end of the Permian period.

FOSSIL FINDERS

The name "Triassic" was given to the period by German **geologist** Friedrich Von Alberti and comes from the three layers ("Tri" = three) in which fossils from this period are found all over the world. These are red beds, then white chalk and black **shales** at the very top. Together they form the "Trias".

Fossil finders, also known as **palaeontologists**, study the marks that previous eras of life on Earth left in the rocks and can build an idea of what the Earth may have looked like in the past. The older the fossil is, the deeper it lies in the geological column.

Help these two palaeontologists uncover this fossil in the Trias by joining the dots in the picture below.

Friedrich Von Alberti
(1795–1878)

Before the Triassic period was the Permian period, when life on Earth was very different. After the Triassic period was the Jurassic period, when dinosaurs became the rulers of the land.

Below is a diagram of part of the history of our Earth. Based on what we said above, can you write into this **geological timeline** *where the Triassic period lies?*

WHEN CROCS RULED THE WORLD!

Pseudosuchians, which means "false crocodiles", were a very successful group of reptiles that evolved in the Early Triassic. They came to dominate the land in the Middle Triassic. At the end of the Triassic, nearly all of them died out leaving just the ancestors of modern day crocodiles and their relatives, alligators and gharials.

Some looked a lot like crocodiles, like **Parasuchus** which ate fish and smaller reptiles, but others looked and lived a lot like dinosaurs and could run on just their back legs, like **Ornithosuchus**. Some pseudosuchians were even vegetarians, like **Stagonolepis** which might have used its upwards-pointing nose to dig up plants, and **Desmatosuchus** which was covered in hard bony plates and spikes for defence whilst it munched through leaves.

Based on the descriptions on the previous page, can you list the names of these pseudosuchians next to their corresponding numbers?

1 _

2 _ _ _ _ _ _ _ _ _ _ _ _ _ _ _ _ _

3 _ _ _ _ _ _ _ _ _ _ _ _ _ _ _ _ _ _ _

4 _ _ _ _ _ _ _ _ _ _ _ _ _ _ _ _ _ _ _

ROAR LIKE A RAUISUCHID

Rauisuchids were the biggest pseudosuchian players on the Late Triassic landscape. They were all predators that could move very quickly. The biggest of them was *Saurosuchus* which was seven metres long. That's four times an average man's height, or the size of a mini-bus! Some of the rauisuchids looked a lot like dinosaurs, except they had a crocodile's body covered in armoured "scutes". Rauisuchids preyed on rhynchosaurs, which were reptiles like **Hyperodapedon**.

This is a Hyperodapedon:

Can you find the 10 *Hyperodapedons* hiding from the rauisuchids in this picture?

THE FIRST DINOSAURS
What makes a dinosaur a dinosaur?

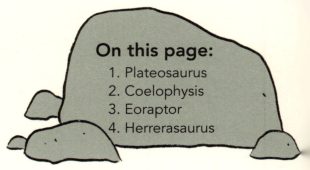
It was not until the Late Triassic period that dinosaurs evolved, but many animals that existed before them looked similar, so why were they not dinosaurs?

The word "dinosaur" comes from Latin and means "terrible lizard" but dinosaurs were actually a different type of reptile to lizards. No dinosaurs swam in the sea or flew in the sky, they all walked around on the ground. Whereas many reptiles have a sprawling or squatting posture – meaning their legs go out to the side of their bodies, like a lizard or a crocodile – dinosaurs had what is called an erect posture. Like modern-day birds – and mammals, just like you – their legs were held directly below their hips.

Some dinosaurs in the Triassic were already growing large – like the herbivorous *Plateosaurus* – but many early dinosaurs like *Eoraptor* and *Procompsognathus* were pretty small compared to their descendants. *Coelophysis* measured around three metres in length, while *Eoraptor* was only about one metre long!

From what you have just found out, which of these four reptiles do you think is a dinosaur?

I love to catch fish.

I chase them around underwater, but like to relax on the shore.

Although I'm very fast under the water, I need to breath air just like other reptiles.

Am I a dinosaur?

☐ Yes ☐ No

I love to catch fish too and I do that by swooping down from the sky.

I can run for a little while on my back legs, but I'm not very stable.

Am I a dinosaur?

☐ Yes ☐ No

I speed around on two legs which are held directly below my hips. This means my arms are free to grab anything I'm hunting.

My teeth are just as sharp as these other guys', but they are more curved and not very good at gripping fish.

Am I a dinosaur?

☐ Yes ☐ No

I'm covered in thick, heavy armour.

My nostrils are very far back on my thin, long snout and, wouldn't you know it, fish are my favourite too.

I don't keep my legs too far under my body, I like to spread out.

Am I a dinosaur?

☐ Yes ☐ No

LEARN TO DRAW TRIASSIC TERRORS

Now that we've learned a lot about the ravenous reptiles that roamed ancient Pangaea, let's try to draw some of them. Follow these basic steps and draw your very own Triassic Terrors.

Draw two pebbles, a large one for the body and a small one for the head.

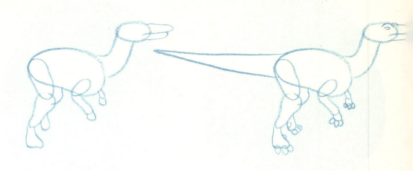

Connect the two pebbles by drawing a long neck and some thin squashed pebbles for legs and arms.

Draw two long pebbles for the snout. For feet and hands, use triangles and squares.

Now you can add the details, like a long tail and some circles for toes and claws.

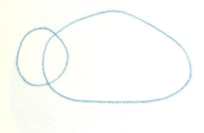

Draw one large rock for the body and a smaller rock for the head.

Add some large, chunky legs by drawing some pebble shapes.

Draw four squashed pebbles for feet. Add some tusks and a mouth.

For toes, draw some small circles. To create a tail, draw a small triangle.

Draw two rocks for the body and the head, then draw two small pebbles for the snout.

Now draw two chunky rocks for the back legs and two thin rocks for the front legs.

Connect the snout to the head and draw four small pebbles for feet.

Finally add a long, swooping tail and some small circles for toes.

You can colour the finished drawings below based on the previous colour pictures in this book, or you can use your imagination and colour them however you like!

COELOPHYSIS

PLACERIAS

SAUROSUCHUS

Predators and Pitfalls : Rules Board

Here are some simple rules that you must follow when playing Triassic Terrors: The Game.

HOW TO PLAY TRIASSIC TERRORS

You are *Eoraptor*, one of the first dinosaurs to exist! One day your relatives and descendants will rule the Earth and grow into giants the likes of which the world will never again see! But the Triassic landscape is not an easy place for the early dinosaurs. There are lots of predators and pitfalls along the way, and before evolving into great, big and fearsome dinosaurs of the Jurassic, your species has to survive. That's up to you!

The aim: *To get to the finish line first, doing your best to avoid the predators and pitfalls.*

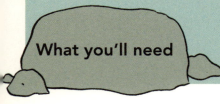

What you'll need

- ONE DIE
- THE RULES BOARD ON THE LEFT

- YOUR FOUR EORAPTOR MARKERS BELOW

- YOUR BRAIN, AND SOME LUCK!

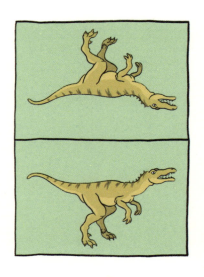

CUT OUT YOUR EORAPTOR MARKERS!

START

FINISH

REMOVABLE
TRIASSIC TERRORS
GAME BOARD!

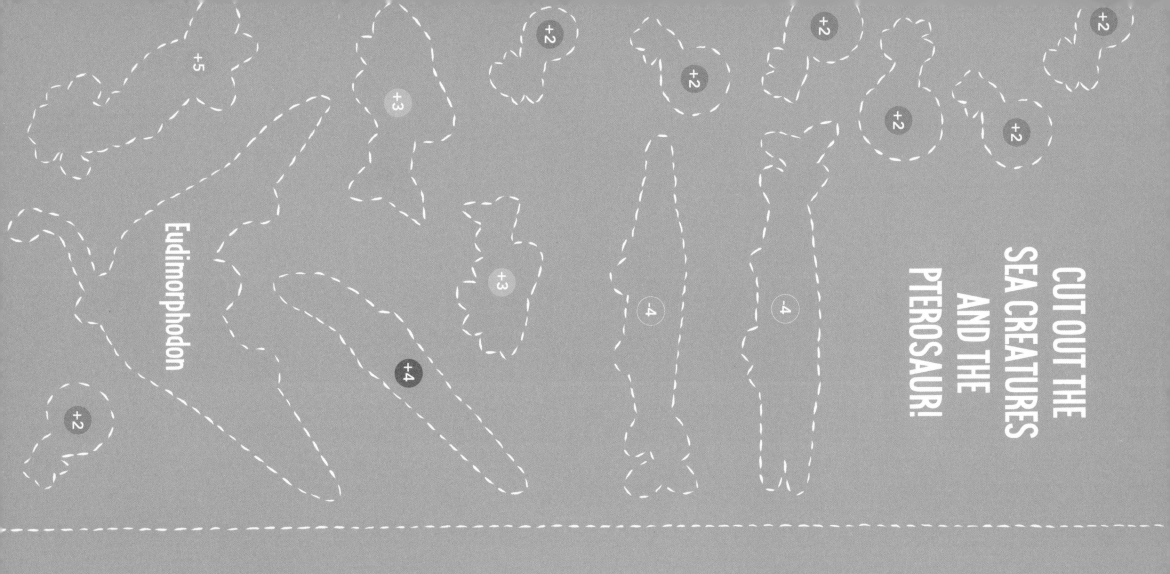

+5

+3

+2

+2

+2

+2

+2

+2

Eudimorphodon

+3

+3

+4

·4·

·4·

**CUT OUT THE
SEA CREATURES
AND THE
PTEROSAUR!**

+2

SEASCAPE

POINTS

BELEMNITE +5
ORTHOCERAS +4
PTERONISCULUS +3
AMMONITE +2
SAURICHTHYS −4

TERRIFIC PTEROSAURS!

Flying high above the pseudosuchians and dinosaurs, the Triassic skies were the first to become home to pterosaurs. Their wings were not made out of feathers, like birds, but from thin skin that stretched out from an incredibly long finger. Although this is like the wings that bats use to fly, pterosaurs' wings only stretched out from one elongated finger, rather than filling the gaps between all of them.

Millions of years later, pterosaurs evolved to be so large some of them had wingspans bigger than a small plane's, but these early flying reptiles were small and had very long tails that might have been used to keep them flying in a straight line. *Eudimorphodon* was one of the earliest pterosaurs and only the size of a small seabird. It probably lived in the same way too, because by studying the shape of its teeth, palaeontologists know it ate fish. Some *Eudimorphodon* fossils have even been found with the remains of a fishy snack inside them where the pterosaur's stomach would have been!

Let's go fishing with pterosaurs!

Early pterosaurs loved fish and tasty molluscs and spent a lot of their time flying over the sea fishing. Help this *Eudimorphodon* get his fishy snacks in time for dinner. Here's how to play...

Cut out all of the creatures and the Triassic seascape on the opposite page.

The aim of the game:
To get as many fish and molluscs (points) as you can without getting bitten by the ferocious Saurichthys!
Each player gets one turn with the pterosaur fishing rod and then passes it on to the next player.
The game ends when all of the tasty sea snacks have been caught.
Then you can tally up the scores and see who won!

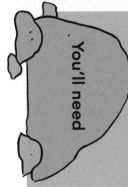

You'll need

- SOME FRIENDS/FAMILY MEMBERS (IT'S BEST TO PLAY THIS GAME WITH TWO OTHERS)
- PAPER CLIPS
- A COCKTAIL STICK
- STRING
- A MAGNET
- YOUR CUT-OUTS AND SEASCAPE
- A NOTEBOOK TO MARK YOUR SCORES
- YOUR TWO HANDS AND SOME LUCK!

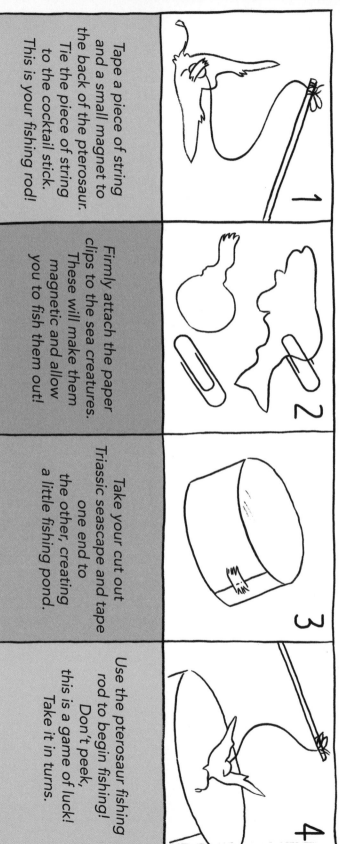

1
Tape a piece of string and a small magnet to the back of the pterosaur. Tie the piece of string to the cocktail stick. This is your fishing rod.

2
Firmly attach the paper clips to the sea creatures. These will make them magnetic and allow you to fish them out!

3
Take your cut out Triassic seascape and tape one end to the other, creating a little fishing pond.

4
Use the pterosaur fishing rod to begin fishing! Don't peek, this is a game of luck! Take it in turns.

UNDER THE SEA IN THE TRIASSIC

What a different world it was under the sea. No whales or dolphins, the long-necked plesiosaurs were just beginning to evolve and even turtles had only recently started to wear shells! Instead, the seas were alive with the first ichthyosaurs, nothosaurs and their relatives, placodonts. Placodonts, like *Placodus* and *Cyamodus*, only lived during the Triassic period. They had large bodies and triangular skulls, which were filled with lots of wide, flat teeth. They used these to crush up shellfish they scraped up off the seabed. Although these had very hard shells just like today, placodonts had enormous muscles attached to their jaws in order to pulverize them and get to the soft animals inside, which could then be ground down and swallowed. Yum!

On this page:
1. Ammonites   5. Belemnites
2. Cyamodus   6. Shonisaurus
3. Placodus   7. Sauricthys
4. Mixosaurus 8. Orthoceras

TANYSTROPHEUS TRICKSTER

Tanystropheus was a very strange marine reptile. At six metres in length it was no small beast, but its formidable three-metre-long neck is what makes this particular creature so confusing. So long and thin was its neck for an animal of such a size that it puzzled palaeontologists for over a century. In the 1850s, Tanystropheus was even wrongly identified as a pterosaur because palaeontologists had confused its very long backbones for wing bones!

Tanystropheus' long neck allowed it to reach into tight spots to get at fish. Help these little fish escape their reptile predators by completing the maze!

ICHTHYOSAUR GALORE

The first ichthyosaurs evolved in the Late Triassic. They were a group of marine reptiles that probably acted just like today's dolphins. By the Jurassic, they had evolved a similar streamlined body shape, with a dolphin-like tail and dorsal fin, which was perfect for cutting through the water very quickly. But in the Triassic, animals like *Chaohusaurus* and *Mixosaurus* still had necks, and long bodies. Early ichthyosaurs could snake their bodies left and right much more than those that evolved later, and they probably hunted fish around shallow seas rather than travelling long distances out in the open ocean. By the Late Triassic, some ichthyosaurs were growing very large indeed, like the enormous *Shonisaurus*.

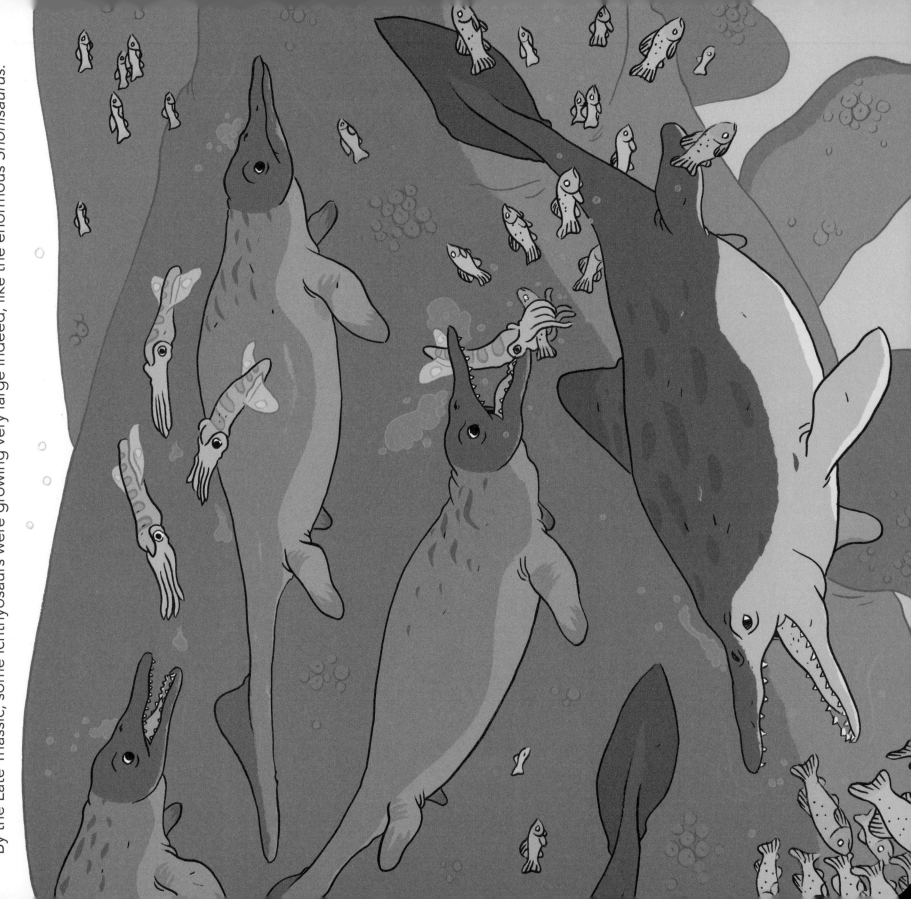

Join the dots above the water line to find out what the *Shonisaurus* was the same size as:

NIMBLE NOTHOSAURS

Nothosaurs were expert marine hunters. With paddle-like hands and feet, streamlined bodies and sharp, interlocking teeth they would make a quick meal out of any fish or squid. However, some scientists think they might have spent a lot of their time out of the water, breeding and sleeping on beaches and rocky outcrops.

Palaeontologists try to work out what prehistoric creatures were like by making comparisons with animals that live today. Clues to behaviour are very rarely left as fossils, so instead we look at the lifestyles and characteristics of animals living today in similar environments.

What animal alive today do you think nothosaurs behaved like?

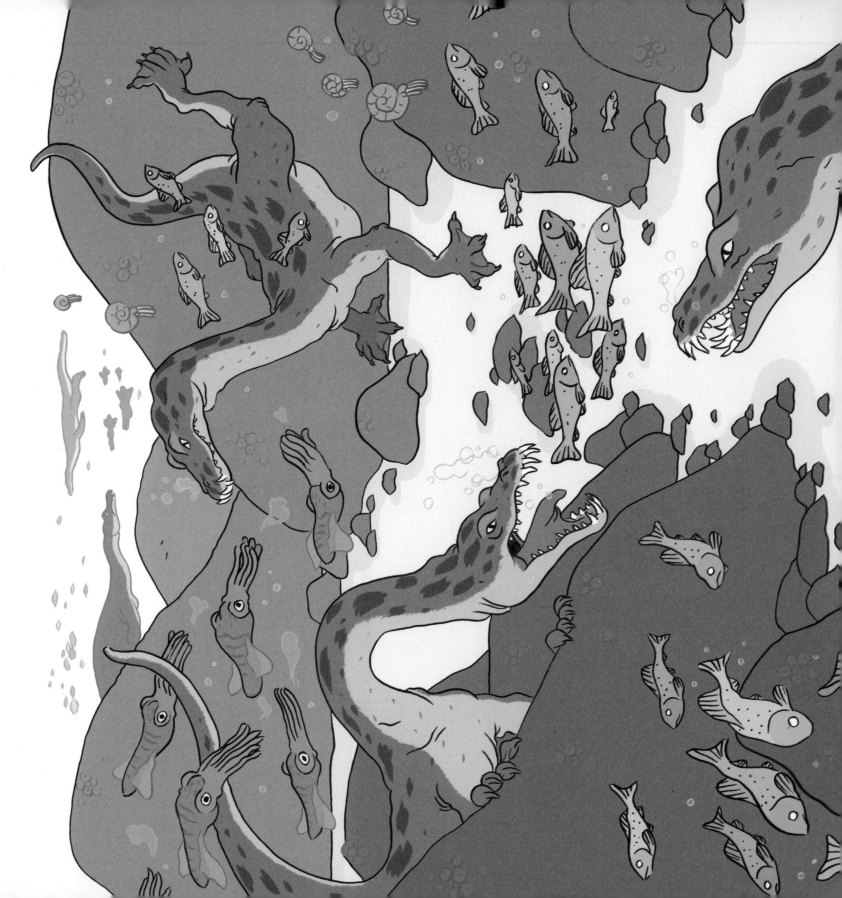

Look at the characteristics and lifestyles of the three animals on this page, which of them most closely resembles those of a nothosaur?

Leopard Seal

▷▷▷ Paddle-like limbs.
▷▷▷ Many different types of teeth in its mouth.
▷▷▷ Gives birth to live young.
▷▷ Very fast in order to hunt speedy prey.
▷ Lives on rocky outcrops, but spends most of its time out at sea.

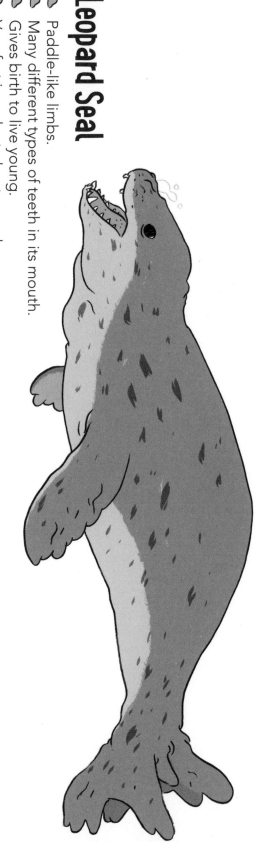

Mako Shark

▷ Teeth are replaced again and again.
▷▷ Skin covered in tooth-like structures.
▷▷▷ Skeleton made of cartilage, not bone.
▷▷▷ Eggs "hatch" inside the mother, who then gives birth to live young.
▷▷▷ Found far away from the coast.

Nile Crocodile

▷▷ Usually slow moving. Ambushes prey!
▷▷▷ Lays eggs out of water.
▷▷▷ All teeth look the same.
▷ Large jaw with a very powerful bite.

WHAT AM I?! FILL IN THE BLANKS...

You have met many fascinating creatures along the journey to discovering Triassic Terrors, now help us fill in the blanks in the exercises on this spread. In palaeontological art (the art of drawing extinct animals), very talented artists often have to fill in gaps in the specimen they are reconstructing. Sometimes they fill in these gaps using details "borrowed" from other fossil specimens, and other times they use descriptions given to them by scientists.

The three animals below are all missing parts too. We need a great young dinosaur artist like you to help us fill in the blanks, using the descriptions next to the animals. Then colour these Triassic Terrors however you want!

Mixosaurus

◁ He has long narrow jaws with lots of sharp teeth in them.
◁ A dolphin-like dorsal fin.
◁ A leaf shaped tail.

Ticinosuchus

◁ She has a series of armoured scutes along her back and tail.
◁ She has many long and sharp teeth in her mouth.

Peteinosaurus

◁ He has lots of small sharp teeth.
◁ A long snapping tail with a leaf shape at the end of it.
◁ He has wings to fly.

Based on these short statements below and what we have learned in the book, can you name these three Triassic Terrors below?

My neck was twice as long as my body and it was very muscular. I confused scientists when I was first discovered, they thought I could fly, but now they think I swam in the sea. Who am I?

I was one of the earliest dinosaurs. I was very light and could have moved very quickly to catch my food. At three metres in length, I was quite a big dinosaur for the Triassic, but nowhere near as big as my Jurassic relatives.

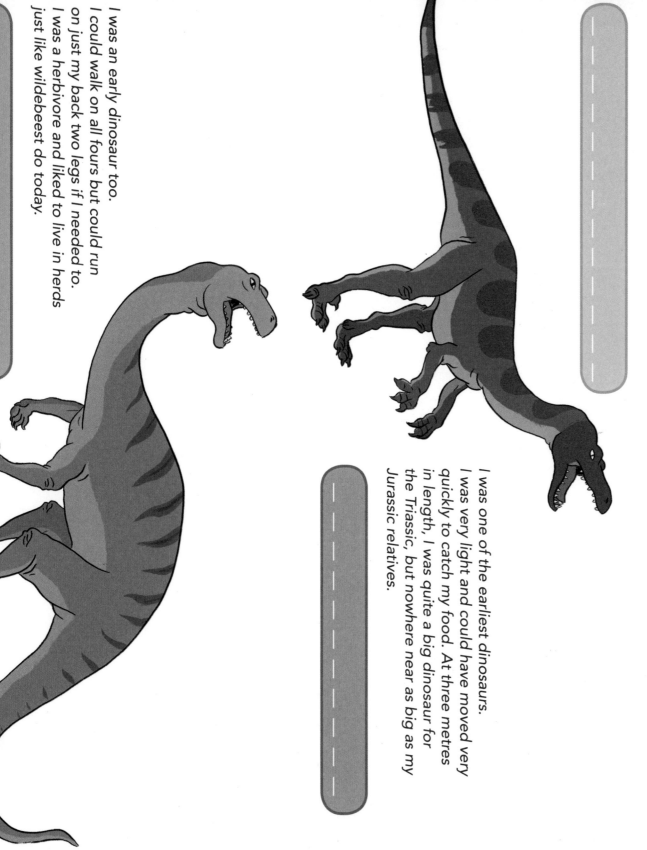

I was an early dinosaur too. I could walk on all fours but could run on just my back two legs if I needed to. I was a herbivore and liked to live in herds just like wildebeest do today.

GLOSSARY OF TERMS

Catastrophic event A very sudden disaster, like a mass extinction.

Climate The climate is the long-term average of the temperature, rainfall, humidity and other things that we usually think makes up the 'weather' for a certain region. Although the weather can change very quickly, the climate is much more stable over time. When the climate of an area changes it can affect what animals and plants can survive.

Dinosaurs A group of reptiles that evolved in the Triassic period and became very successful in the Jurassic. Although most of them became extinct at the end of the Cretaceous period, some small forms survived and evolved into modern-day birds.

Dorsal fin A fin on an animal's back. These have evolved in ichthyosaurs, whales, dolphins and sharks.

Era One of the ways geologists split up the huge amounts of time they think about. An era is not as long as an eon, but it is longer than a period.

Erect Posture The way dinosaurs and some other animals hold their leg bones. If the leg bones are not held in an erect posture, they stick out to the side in a 'sprawling' fashion.

Evolution explains how changes occur over time in the average sizes, shapes and behaviours of a population of living things. This happens because some individuals are more successful at breeding and passing on their characteristics to future generations. This process of 'natural selection' explains the appearance of biodiversity over great spans of geological time.

Geologist Geology is one of the oldest sciences. It is the study of the Earth by investigating rocks. A geologist might study the history of life, how the Earth has coped with changing climates or understanding why volcanoes erupt and when earthquakes strike.

Gorgonopsids Predators related to the ancestors of mammals. They had enormous teeth that looked like those used by sabre-toothed cats. They were widespread before the mass extinction event at the end of the Permian.

Ichthyosaurs Marine reptiles that first appeared in the Triassic. They probably behaved in a similar way to today's dolphins.

Mammals Animals with hair, large brains, a single jaw bone and three small ear bones. Some of the very earliest mammals, such as *Morganucodon*, evolved during the Triassic period.

Marine Lives in the sea.

Mass Extinction Very rare events when a large proportion and variety of life on Earth becomes extinct. The types of animals that become successful after a mass extinction are often different to those that were successful immediately before.

Mesozoic An era of time that lasted from the beginning of the Triassic period until the end of the Cretaceous.

Meteorite A piece of material such as rock that hits the Earth from space. Most of the time these burn up in the atmosphere. When this happens, they are called meteors.

Nothosaurs Long-necked marine reptiles that had the same ancestors as the plesiosaurs that swam under the Jurassic oceans.

Palaeontologist Someone that studies fossils in order to learn about animals that are no longer alive today. Palaentologists need to be good at science, geography and spending a lot of time outdoors.

Pangaea The name palaeontologists use to describe the massive landmass that existed during the Triassic. It was surrounded by a single ocean - Panthalassa - and began to separate in the Jurassic period.

Panthalassa The great ocean that surrounded Pangaea during the Triassic period.

Period A shorter amount of time than an era, but still millions of years long. Periods are defined by the types of rocks that were laid down during them, and the fossils found within them.

Permian The period before the Triassic that lasted from around 300 to 250 million years ago. Reptiles and some synapsids became extremely successful in the many deserts that appeared across Pangaea during this time.

Placodonts Aquatic reptiles that lived in shallow waters during only the Triassic period. They were covered in bony plates to protect them from predators and they ate molluscs like bivalves.

Plesiosaurs Marine reptiles that had long necks and became very successful in the Jurassic period.

Predator Animals that hunt and eat other animals.

Pseudosuchians A group of reptiles that were successful before the dinosaurs. Crocodiles and their relatives are the only pseudosuchians alive today.

Pterosaurs A group of reptiles that were able to glide and fly thanks to thin skin that stretched backwards from a very long finger. Pterosaurs later evolved to be the largest flying creatures of all time and some grew long crests on their heads.

Rauisuchids A group of predatory pseudosuchians. Like other extinct pseudosuchians they were more closely related to crocodiles than dinosaurs.

Reptiles Animals with scaly skin that lay eggs out of water. The Triassic Terrors were all reptiles and so were dinosaurs; modern reptiles include crocodiles, snakes, lizards and turtles.

Rhynchosaurs These were herbivorous animals that were incredibly successful during the Early Triassic. The front of their skull acted like long scissor-like teeth and some of them had digging claws on their hind legs. Palaeontologists think one reason they disappeared was because the type of fern they fed on became extinct during the Middle Triassic.

Scutes The hard, bony parts of some animals' skin. Crocodiles alive today have skin covered in scutes.

Shale A type of rock that is formed out of ancient mud. It often splits into very thin layers.

Species The word scientists use to group types of animals together.

Supercontinent A massive area of land like Pangaea. These are made out of continents that later split apart and become separated by oceans. Another supercontinent, Rodinia, existed about 1 billion years ago.

Synapsid Synapsids include mammals, along with their ancestors and relatives, like Dimetrodon. Most fossil synapsids usually have one hole in their skull behind their eye, although this hole is closed up in mammals.

Terrestrial Lives on the ground.

Vertebrates Any animal that has a backbone (a 'vertebral column'). Most of the animals you have met in Triassic Terrors are kinds of vertebrates.

TRIASSIC CHEAT SHEET!

Q. Can you list the names of these **Pseudosuchians** next to their corresponding numbers?

Answers:
1. Desmatosuchus
2. Parasuchus
3. Stagonolepis
4. Ornithosuchus

PAGES 5&6

Q. Am I a dinosaur?
A. Eoraptor – YES!

PAGE 10

START
FINISH

PAGE 22

Q. Can you name the three Triassic Terrors?

Answers:
1. Plateosaurus
2. Coelophysis
3. Tanystropheus

PAGE 28

QUATERNARY
NEOGENE
PALEOGENE
CRETACEOUS
JURASSIC
TRIASSIC
PERMIAN
CARBONIFEROUS
DEVONIAN
SILURIAN
ORDOVICIAN
CAMBRIAN

CENOZOIC
MESOZOIC
PALEOZOIC

PAGE 4

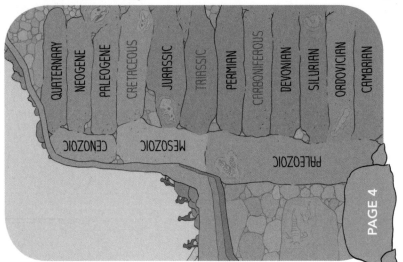

Find the ten Hyperodapedons

PAGES 7&8

Q. What animal alive today did the **nothosaur** behave like?
A. Leopard seal.

PAGE 26

PAGE 3

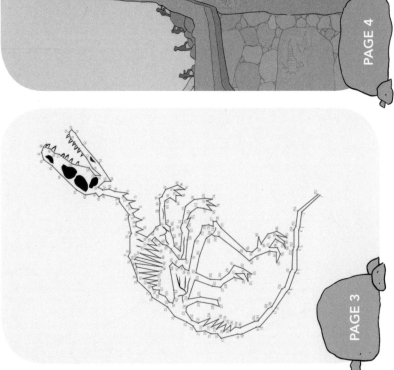

A Viking ship!

PAGE 24